DESTINED TO FLY

Unleashing Your Greatness

Chidi C. ObiGod

Amazon

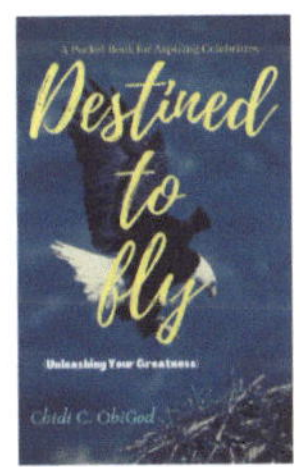

CONTENTS

ACKNOWLEDGEMENTS

Thanks to my parent eagles. John and Elizabeth Enemuo.
Amaka Onyechere (late)
Bishop T. D. Jakes
Pastor Chris Oyakhilome
Max Lucado
Anthony Robbins
Brian Tracy
Mark Zuckerberg
Lionel Messi
Dwayne Johnson
Chinenye I. Ubah
And many more not mentioned here. You guys have imparted my life directly and indirectly.

DESTINED

TO

FLY

INTRODUCTION

Ostrich is a giant among bird yet it can't fly. Penguin is a beauty among birds yet it can't fly either. Nightingale is a bird with beautiful songs and it flies but not as high as the eagle.

Flight is a destiny and not all birds have such a destiny. High flying is also a destiny. Whatever you are destined to do, you are designed for that purpose. You have the characteristics that helps you do what you are destined to do. Ostrich has long legs that help it run 70 km/h on a plain land. Penguins have flaps and a body shape that helps them swim 12 km/h in the water. Nightingale has a vocal cord that enables it sing those beautiful songs. Then eagles have wings that helps them fly and dive at speeds of 201 – 322 km/h. That's impressive!

If you are destined to fly but you find yourself running in the plain, you will never taste satisfaction. If you are destined to soar and you find yourself swimming in the sea, you will never feel fulfilled. The sky will always be calling you. Destiny will always be calling out to you and until you respond to it you will never be satisfied.

If you are destined to be a celebrity, living in obscurity will always frustrate you. The instinct to rise and fly to where you will be celebrated will always be stirring you on the inside until you respond to it.

If you are an eagle, you cannot compare yourself with ostrich and penguins it is an insult to your destiny. You must embrace your uniqueness. Utilize and maximize your abilities.

This book is for those who aspire to spend their life in the limelight. Those who want to be used as icon at a particular field in life. Those who wants to be famous and great in what they do. Anybody can become famous in any field of their endeavor. But I also find out that greatness is a calling. Not everybody has that calling as much as you think everybody does. Some have the ability to fly but not very high, while some are destined and gifted to fly very high and until they get to that great height in life they will never feel fulfilled.

Great people are not satisfied at certain levels in life. They don't accept what is below their calling. Where a mediocre builds a paradise, the great one builds a step. He knows what he wants and doesn't settle for anything less. Put him in a cage and give him everything he wants he will still rebel to taste freedom.

Nothing is wrong with you each time you look up and feel compelled to be like these famous and great people, something in you is linked to them. Don't ignore the desires and passions to do some certain things. You have a connection with anything that compels you.

As you embark on your journey as a high flyer, this small book will serve as your hand book and road map to get to the place of your destiny.

LITTLE WINGS

I want to fly far and high
Make my podium in the sky
Build my next in Jupiter
Like a star I want to glitter.

But my little wings I still neglect
For it can't compete with the great.
So I've accused myself with excuses
And let my abilities wither in abuses.

Comfortably scratching the grounds
With chickens, as slackness abounds;
Yet the eagle's voice keeps calling
To escape that life too appalling.

How I wish I have bigger wings
To soar high along with king;
Yet I'll use these wings of mine,
They will get stronger with time.

Stretch them according to my age
And throw myself off the edge.
The fear's gone, now I rise and fly;
I'm just brave enough to try.

CHAPTER 1.

PECK YOUR WAY OUT

In the kingdom of all that flies, eagles stand out. Beautiful. Majestic. Magnificent and glorious. He is called the king of the sky the same way the lion is called the king of the jungle. Apart from vultures their scavenging cousins, eagle is larger than other raptors. Length 71-96 cm. Weight 3000-6300g. Wingspan 204 cm. Bald eagle has heavy body, large head, long, hooked bills and extremely sharp eyes. Many empires, kingdoms and nations use eagle as a symbol. Ranging from Roman empire to United States of America, you will see it in the coat of arm of the most populated African nation Nigeria. Eagle is a symbol of excellence, power, freedom, beauty, honour, grace and leadership.

This bird that has fascinated and inspired us over the years don't just appear from a thin air. His journey to excellence and power began somewhere insignificant, a place of obscurity inside a white shell laying on a nest. Like most birds, eagle's life begins inside an egg laid by its mother.

Except you are a zoologist or an expert in animal rearing you cannot recognize an eagle's egg among other eggs because bald eagle's eggs are white in colour, shaped like most eggs, range from 6-8 cm long and 5-6 cm wide, weighing 110-130 grams. So it is like normal bird's egg except that what's inside is unique and special.

In the same way, there may not be anything special about where you start in life. You may start at the same common place where everyone else started - the same local neighbourhood or community setting, attended the same local school, worshipped in the local religious center. You don't need a special background to be special in life. You don't need to attend an extraordinary elementary school to believe you have an extraordinary destiny.

Great eagle, the high flyer started the same way sparrows, pigeons, chickens and other small birds started, from an egg lying on the floor of a hazy nest, enclosed in the same white or blown shell. So stop thinking that those who fly far and high have a special, extraordinary background that you lack.

Many successful people and celebrities of our time who are high flyers in their various fields started from a grounded background but they didn't allow that background to keep their back on the ground.

Ralph Lauren is a high flyer in fashion world, but he was once the youngest egg of a poor Jewish immigrants in America. According to his high school year book his goal in life was to be a millionaire. He is the owner of the Polo fashion line.

Dolly Parton is a high flyer and icon of country music, but she used to be a beautiful pretty egg in a one-room cabin in the woods of Locust Ridge in Tennessee. While she was growing up, lack of money was always a problem in her family.

Omotola Jolade Ekeinde is a Nigeria super star who has a fulfilling career. She once made it to the list of Time's Magazine list of the Most Influential People in the world 2003. In an interview, she once sighted how her glowing up was.

"Once, my mother and I went to beg for money in the house of one prominent Nigerian. We were so totally hopeless that day. I have never told anybody this before. We cried all day because my younger brothers school fees were due and we didn't have money to pay."

So when you look at where you are lying as a helpless egg in the dirt of poverty, stained by dark shits of lack. Remember you are not the first to be there. You are not the first to be born into a poor family. You are not the first to be raised up by a single parent. You are not the first to come out of a broken home. It is a common place for high flyers. Not all kings were born in the palace, some were born in the manger. You don't get to decide how you come into this world, where you would be born, the family you would be born into. Some found themselves as princes and princess in a royal family, some found themselves as loyal peasants by the country side. Some were born into affluence while some were born into penury.

So remember that no high flyer falls from the sky, most of them kicked off from a rough and rugged place. Some greatness you see started from a small beginning of an embryo in an egg and the worst of it all is that you are a seed inside a shell, and nobody will celebrate who you are until you break out of the shell. But you can't break out of the shell until you are incubated.

SIT ON ME

All you need as an embryo in a shell is a parent eagle that will sit on you till you hatch. You are a seed or an embryo without form. And if you must take the right shape and form you need the help of parent eagles.

Life starts with successful fusion of sperm and egg called fertilization. The formative time of your life is very crucial. You are a greatness in making, a king or queen in preparation. Every king was once a kid so every eagle was once an eaglet, and every butterfly was once a caterpillar.

Never neglect the days of your humble beginning. At the early stage of your life your future may not look predictable yet no eyes have seen, no ears have heard and no imagination has conceived what the future holds in store for you. So don't be surprise if some people see you at the egg stage of your life and consider you to be lifeless shell or a baseless ball they can kick around, push you from one corner to another. They may reject you because they don't know it is a high flyer that resides inside.

The colour of the egg doesn't matter neither the size or weight of it. It doesn't matter if the shell, your container has some dark spots, pumps and rough edges. What matters is your content, the personality on the inside. And you need people who will see beyond the shell and value what lies within. When others push you away, they will roll you close and sit on you to incubate your potentials till it hatches.

Parent eagles don't sit on you to hinder you; they sit on you that you may take form. They brood on your mind till you form the right mentality, philosophy and values. Your thoughts, words, actions, habits and character need to take the right form because they sum up your destiny.

Parent eagles may be your biological parents, as well they are mentors, role models, teachers, life coaches and masters. They provide the right information that gives form to your destiny and instructions that construct your identity. They give your life direction, visions and education. They create the right environment for you to hatch. They raise the temperature till the shell cracks. If the environment is too cold, you may stay in the raw state forever and if it is too hot it can kill you so they make the environment conducive for you to hatch. You may not like their words of instructions, because you consider it harsh or mean but believe me it is for your good. You may accuse them of being abusive but if you desire to remain elusive you need their touch of discipline. What you call harsh can be what will hatch you.

Sometimes you choose your mentors sometimes your mentors choose you, but don't forget it is not everybody that has the qualification to be your mentor because some will eat you raw. Out there are egg-eaters who feasts on the destinies and potentials of young people they should help to manifest. And one sure way you should recognize these egg-eaters is that they are selfish, self-centered, who put their satisfaction and gratification first.

Some will not eat you but out of jealousy they will sit on you till they crush you and make sure you never ever emerge. They are afraid of what you will become and insecure that you will rise and be greater than them. So beware of those who eat up what they should heat up and those who harm what they should warm up till it hatches.

The right mentors understand you more and they are comfortable with your great destiny. They know they are not giving you anything that you don't have but helping you discover and develop yourself. They help you develop the little vision you already have till it is big enough and point you to the right direction. So submit yourself to their grace, stay under their coverage and tutorage.

PECK YOUR WAY OUT

While you are confined inside the shell, restricted by forces you don't know, a time will come when instinct will tell you like an alarm clock, 'It's time to break out'. This happens when what used to be comfortable before becomes uncomfortable. When you come to that awareness that you are stuck in something that is limiting you.

You cannot move out of the shell if you don't feel confined, suffocating and frustrated. It will hit you like an awakening call that the shell that once gave you nourishment is no longer needed by you. The shell is a small world but it can never be compared to this larger world where your limit of flying is infinite. Don't be stuck in the small world, break out of it.

I know nobody decides how he or she comes into this world. You don't get to decide or choose where you are born and how you are born into this world. It is not fair that some people are formed in the beautiful womb and on the day of their delivery, a bed was laid for them in white sheets, the theater is set before their arrival, they have a mother who would push them out into the careful latex gloved hand of a mid-wife who would smile at their arrival. Unfortunately some destinies don't come into this world like that, they were stuck in shell and for them to emerge they must peck their way out.

It may be a shell of family norms, shell of religious dogmas, shell of traditional beliefs, shells of cultural illiteracy that limits your freedom and creativity, and you must get out of it. It starts by thinking outside of the shell, when you start to question old beliefs, ideologies, doctrines and philosophies that seem to confine your vast mind, your emancipation is at hand. Some truisms are not true. Some old clichés may sound good but not right for you. You must learn when you outgrow certain stages of your life. One of the major signs that you have out grown the shell is when the shell is uncomfortable and frustrating for you. What once brought you provisions and protections can turn out to be a limitation as you grow bigger in life.

Don't wait for the shell to crack, it may not. Nobody may come to crack it for you. You have to a stage that you should no expect a sage to lay his hand on you or call you out for you to emerge. Stop waiting for someone to pour holy oil on you and crack your shell with stones of his creeds and decrees for you to emerge. It requires your own pecking from the inside to bring yourself out. So either you peck your way out or you remain trapped in the shell for a long time. The way out is inside out not outside in.

From the inside, you peck your way out. You read your way out. Think your way out. Meditate your way out. Pray your way out. Confess your way out. Create your way out. Plan your way out. Fight your way out. Whichever way you want to use to stick your head out, use it just make sure you are out of that limitation.

Don't let anything hold you back. You have been stuck in the shell for long and it is becoming a hell in a cell for you. The world is waiting for you. I heard that the stages of France are waiting to watch you dance. The streets of Singapore are eager to hear you sing. British institutions await your graduation to have you teach and reach out to those out of their royal reach. China towns have their eyes in the sky to see you shine as star. The citizens of Los Angeles longs to have you as their legal angel of rescue. If you lag behind we the Lagos people will continue to lack a quality leader you are destined to be. You are the new sensation of Hollywood, Bollywood or Nollywood. A new revelation in sports world. A paradigm in the technology world.

So get unstuck from whatever shell that is covering you. Unstuck yourself from your past, your old habits and normalcy. Peck your way out. Stick your head out of your comfortable shell despite how attached you are with your shell; your destiny is in the sky not the shell. Step out of the shell to the nest because the nest is a better place to stay.

CHAPTER 2.

FROM NEST TO NATURE

The nest is meant to conceal you while you grow. It is your nursery where you are groomed till a whole lot of things grow in your life. In the nest, your vision develops, your perception matures and your feathers thicken.

In the nest the eaglet learns what it means to be an eagle especially by watching, listening and responding to instinct and guidance of parent eagles. In the same way the nest is the school where you learn the ways and lifestyles of high flyers. There your appetite grows. You move from feeding on milk or yolks to feeding on flesh. At the same time, you learn what to feed on and what to despise because some things will make you grow up and some will make you throw up.

I know how eager you are to go out there and see the world but I must break it to you. Wait till you are ready. I know you have abilities but don't rush them, give yourself the time to grow. If you are going too fast, you will slip. Never be in a haste to manifest, it could be dangerous. Rather sit back and watch parent eagles. You have a lot to learn from them. Feed on what they give you till you have learnt how to hunt for yourself.

You are not only born great. Greatness must be born and formed in you. Have the patience to sit in the nest and learn.

When a young immature eagle looks at older full grown eagles their beautiful white head and tails (as in bald eagle species), their dark blown bodies and wings, bright yellow bills and legs, he may be in a haste to grow and reach plumage because his head and tails are dark, his wings brown, with bodies mottled with white in varying amounts. Yet he must wait because to attain adult full plumage takes time.

No matter how you admire successful and famous people for what they have achieved and acquired you must understand that it took them time to come to such a place. You may think that you are ready but you are not. No matter how you stretch your wings if it is not ready for flight you won't make it. Develop your vision and perception. Allow your feathers to grow. Sharpen your bills and talons.

I made a mistake of launching very early in my life when I was not fully prepared. Though I had a mother eagle who provided me protection and I flew under her shadow. While I was enjoying what I was not ready for a tragedy happened. She flew out one day and she never returned, she was shot out of the sky. That's when it became very clear to me that I was not matured enough to leave the nest for nature.

To be famous or very successful early in life without having a parent eagle to guide and protect you is very dangerous. You may think you have it all figured out but believe me you don't. So embrace the nest and let these things grow in your life.

1. **VISION**: The eagle vision is one of the strongest in the animal kingdom. An adult eagle's eyes are as big as that of a human being but 4 to 8 times stronger and sharper

than that of the average human. An eagle can spot a rabbit 3.2 km away. They have strong colour vision with resolution and clarity. Their eyes are so important that it is larger in size than their brain. Your vision is your greatest asset because it decides your direction and target in life. Make sure you know what you want in life and how you want it. Be observant and accurate. Remember that little things matter. Develop the ability to pick a target and focus on that target. While in the nest see yourself beyond the nest, beyond your present circumstances. Learn to project into the future and see yourself in the future doing what the fully grown you will be doing. Your small apartment may be your nest, see yourself beyond that, beyond your outrageously poor neighbourhood. Dream of the mountain top, dream of soaring above the cloud. Don't allow where you are and what you see at the moment cloud your vision. You are a creature of vision so while you are in the nest let your vision develop.

2. **BEAKS**: Eagles have sharp curved bills which they used initially to peck their way out of the shell and as they mature and hunt they use it to hold and tear flesh. Your destiny may be tied to your mouth. Remember it is your mouth you used to peck your way out, you will still use it to feed yourself, so sharpen it and make it stronger. Use it to hunt not to hurt yourself by saying things that are contrary to your destiny. Your word is like a sword, wield it well to your advantage not to your disadvantage. Develop a prayer life. A positive confession life. An affirmative life. Become better in communicating with yourself and efficient in communicating with others. Your talent may be in your mouth that through what you say you get paid in the sense that your career or profession deals with communication as a television

presenter, radio anchor, sales person, public speaker, preacher, vocalist, you must sharpen this area of your life. You must sharpen your communication abilities. Remember your mouth is another powerful asset.

3. **TALONS:** The day I know eagles are exceptionally strong is the day I watched a video Clip on YouTube where an eagle preyed on a young wolf. It just dived down and picked that young wolf in an unbelievable way. How good can you grasp stuffs? Eagles use their claws to grasp firmly. As a high flyer your grasping ability must be strong. As a hunter you will pick something at a lower level and take it up to a higher level, and if you don't grasp well you will lose your game on your way up. Nothing comes easy. The things you want in life may not be delivered to your door step like a box of pizza. You have to hunt. Your ability to grasp well determines how successful you will be as a hunter. You grasp an idea or inspiration, you must have the ability to hold on to it and take it higher to where it is useful. For example, your ability to grasp an idea and carry it up can help you write a great book. Your ability to grasp a mental picture can help you in acting or producing a movie or paint an abstract piece of art work. Your technical ability helps you invent a great master piece. You need a strong head-hand coordination. Make sure you develop any skill of creativity you have. You must be someone who holds on to things and don't easily let go of worthwhile things. People that lack this ability easily let go of jobs, relationships, projects and opportunities that should sustain them. Your ability to hold on to what is helpful and useful is very essential for your survival. Sharpen your talons to fight off any challenge or resistance that will come to scare you off from what you have worked so hard to kill.

4. **FEATHERS:** We live in a cold world and to survive you need to stay warm. Initially parents eagles cover you and provide you with warmth till your feathers grow and thicken. They provide you with the love, faith and hope that warm the heart because you need the affection of people in this cold world. You need someone to lean on when you are weak. You need friends who provide you warmth with their closeness and affection especially during the winter season of life. Value whoever that's there to give you warmth. But remember you can't live your entire life depending on their close relationship to survive, you must survive this cold world on your own by growing your own feathers which provides you with warmth. You have to give yourself internal warmth. Love yourself, give yourself hope and faith. Internalize your love, faith and hope. Don't always expect to get them externally. Feathers give you the ability to fly. Make yourself flyable. Don't make your feathers heavy but lighter. Let go of things that will not make you flyable. Don't always let things stick to you. Forgive people that needs to be forgiven. Have a light heart always by staying happy. Heavy hearts hardly fly.

ENEMY IN THE NEST

To every life on earth there is a predator. They wear camouflage and move unnoticed as insurgency soldiers. Predators like naïve and harmless preys because to them, it is easier. You don't have to fly around to draw attention, you don't have to raise voice over the hills and soar the mountain peaks to make your presence known. Predators can pick your scent while you are sitting helpless in the nest. Like star gazers from afar they know when an eagle is born. They won't come at you because you have made a hundred kills. They will come at you because you are a potential enemy. They know that the young shall grow and they can't risk it to see you grow. They are afraid that you will grow bigger, fly over their head and they will be under your shadow. So they will crawl up to your nest to kill you in your crib.

Have you ever wondered why strange things happened to you while you were growing up? I mean strange things that would have claimed your life or destroyed you entirely like being abused or raped. Traumas, congenital defects, ailments, spiritual attacks, accidents and incidents that are not coincidence. All these are acts of predators sent as terminators from the future to terminate you in the present. Does that scare you?

Welcome to nature. Nature is beautiful but nature has beasts that hides in the dark crevices to attack the helpless. Don't panic because what can't kill you can only make you stronger. What you are afraid of now will one day be afraid of you. What comes to eat you now will be something you will grow to eat in the future.

Remember you have a parent eagle and you are not alone. Invoke their help. Don't fight it on your own. It may be the virus of depression, the constricting serpent of frustration, the boa of obsession that's trying to eat you up in secret. Cry out for help. You need spiritual protection from spiritual attacks. You need emotional support for emotional attack, consult a psychologist or psychiatrist whenever darkness comes to arrest your mind or molest your body. I repeat. Don't die in silence. Call out for help. No matter how far the parent eagles are, they will fly back to your rescue.

While in the nest, the enemy may not succeed in snatching you away but may succeed in snatching away the ones sitting close to you. I have watched the enemies snatch away my friends and classmates while I was growing up and it was very traumatic as well. I lost an age mate, classmate and playmate at the age of 12. He was very smart and sharp but his little developing life was terminated by the sharp machete of Bakassi boys (the then notorious vigilante groups who executed their convicts by cutting them into pieces and set them ablaze).

At 16, I lost another best friend and name sake to the bullets of terminators who many claimed to be a rival cult gang. I still remember the visions we shared together few weeks before he was gunned down.

I know three of my secondary school classmates who didn't make it to the university with others. They died after our high school graduation.

I don't know your story but I am sure you must have escaped the hand of the terminator once, twice or times you can't count. It doesn't mean you are more special or more gifted. It is the mercy of God that keeps you.

THE HUNTER'S CAGE

Out there are hunters who seek to trap you and cage you for sports. They don't come to kill like enemies. They come as friends or employers with lots of promises and attractive offers. They play on your innocence and inexperience. They have seen your potentials so they want you solely for their own gain and to your own pain. They promise you a better life in a silver or golden cage. They are only interested in the songs you sing if you are a song bird. They want to make merchandise of your feathers.

These hunters will take advantage of the absence of your parent eagle and climb into your nest and steal you away to their cage. They pay you daily, weekly or monthly enough to keep you alive for their gratification.

No matter what they give or pay you in their cage it can never be compared to what you will achieve when you are free and hunting for yourself. If you are a girl eagle, a lot of men will try to lure you to their cage where you will forfeit your dreams and aspirations. Where you will never be free to be the woman you are destined to be. Remember you are a high flyer not a parrot, nightingale or chicken. A lady parrot can be comfortable in those golden cages and a hen doesn't mind being confined in a silver cage laying endless eggs but as an eagle you are, the cage is not for you. So don't let anything or anyone cage you, no matter how much they give and pay you

CHAPTER 3.

REACH FOR YOUR NICHE

There's this story of a farmer who climbed a mountain in search of mountain herbs, there he found an eagle's nest on a tree in the mountain, so he took one of the egg and brought it to his farm, placed the egg with other eggs of his chicken so that they should be hatched together.

Good for him, the eaglet hatched out with other chicks and he had to live with the chickens he hatched out with. He lived with his chicken siblings, ate what they were eating, and did whatever they were doing. It squawked, squeaked and scratched the ground with them.

Even though it lived with them, among them and like them, along the line it began to notice it was different. Somehow it noticed its visions are better and farther, his talons are longer, his feathers are bigger, his yellow bills are sharper and curved. It noticed that what other chicks found hard to do, are easier with him. But how could it explain that?

In the poultry, the turkeys would spread their wings, bragged around but couldn't fly. The chickens had acrophobia. But each time he spread his wings he felt something lifting it. Every time it decided to embrace its uniqueness that it was distinct, its siblings, friends and peers would start to treat it like a freak and a mix-fit. It was always misunderstood. In order to blend in with them, it chose not to be himself anymore but to be like them.

This is the story of some high flyers reading this. You grew up different from others. Either by error of omission or commission your destiny was derailed and relocated early in life. You started life with the wrong foot, surrounded by people who are not your kind and they don't help matters. Talking about parent eagles sound strange to you because you know you don't have one and never had. You were raised by a hen instead of an eagle. You were raised in an orphanage home and moved from one foster home to another. You grew up in a ghetto and slum.

Even when some of those people noticed you are special and different, they did nothing to help you. When you are with your friends hanging out in the neighborhood and you tell them that you can fly far, they look at you and tell you, "You are crazy." Even when instinct makes you spread your wings to give flying a try, they tell you "Knock it off. We've tried it before, we couldn't do and you can't." If you persist in your desires they have a way of clipping your wings out of jealousy by telling you, "Who do you think you are?"

Staying with chickens for long can make you lose your identity because your association defines you. You can be an eagle but people think you are a chicken because you are always seen with chickens. One of the greatest influences in your life is people you associate with. The friends you keep can decide whether you will fly or spend your life crawling. Circumstances beyond your control may have placed you among chickens and you may not know exactly who you are but hold on to that belief that you are different.

CATERPILLAR EXPERIENCE

Have you ever thought that your life is awkward? Unlike the eagle mentioned above you don't see anything special or unique about you. You can't predict your own future because you don't know what will become of you with time. People say you have a life expectancy of dying very young or going to jail before the age of 25. You see yourself as a loser because nobody loves you and the people around act as if they don't see the need of you being around. You were marked to be wasted. Did you ever feel like that? So did a caterpillar.

When caterpillar comes out of its egg, it doesn't look like something that has a destiny. It looks absurd, detestable and offensive. There is no way you can look at a caterpillar and predict its destiny unlike the way you can predict the destiny of the eaglet in the nest.

Caterpillar is a worm, not just a worm but a pest yet it has a future. It is not admired by anyone, not wanted in the environment it grows. It is on the hit list to be hand-picked for destruction because no one wants a waster.

Some people's life is like that of the caterpillar. They are the caterpillar of the family, the one that will not amount to anything who wastes family resources. The caterpillar of the neighborhood, every parent tells their kids to avoid him that he is a poisonous worm. He is the spoiled brat by the street. In the class he is the least likely to succeed. He is the F-student in the midst of A-students just like Ben Carson. Or the mental retard like Albeit Einstein who couldn't speak well till the age of 9. He is the kid with autism. The short, stubby and stupid kid in school sports field.

Caterpillar experience is a painful experience. It is when people look down on you because of your present predicaments. When you are sacked from your job because they think you are not good enough. They say you are slow and sluggish. They say you are too fat to be used. They call you ugly, good for nothing, pathetic and disgusting. They never see anything good in you. As a boy you can't have the hot girls you are attracted to because they look at you as a poor worm.

Just the same way some caterpillars have pikes on their body; you have some annoying habits that push people away from you. They hate you because they don't understand you. They think you stink with body odours, foul breathe, they laugh at your face cursed with temporal acnes and pimples.

Do you in anyway relate to what I said above? Have you ever felt that there's nothing special and unique about you? You don't think you have any gift or talent compared to your friends. When you compare yourself with them you see yourself as a retard that is backward in life. Where others seem to be flying, running or walking over, you notice you are just crawling through.

One thing I want to tell you is this – Don't hate yourself. It doesn't matter who hates you, who rejects you and gave up on you, don't give up on yourself. Hang on, you will surely turn out to be something beautiful and colorful. I wish you will see how beautiful your future is. Despite you have been hurt and rejected by people who supposed to accept and love you. It doesn't matter what they said and how they treated you as a liability. Forgive them because they do not see what the future holds for you. Neither do they know what destiny has in store for you.

FEED ON GREENS

There's one thing you must do to survive the caterpillar stage of your life. Feed on greens. Caterpillar eats the green leaves they were born unto. Discover your niche and feed on them. Your niche is that place where you feel at home, where something in you comes alive.

Green is the colour of life and nature. Don't disconnect yourself from nature and its beauty. Daily feed your mind with inspirational materials. Listen to great music that inspires you (those kinds of music that transcends nice sounds but the ones that touch your inner mind and spirit). Admire great pieces of art, drawings, paintings and scruptures. Let nature speak to you through the early morning songs of birds, rays of the sun, the wave of the sea. Feed on what gives you life, what calls out the artist or scientist in you, what awakens the genius in you.

Find that thing that inspires and motivates you then feed on it. Consume as much as you need. Anthony Robbins said he read over 700 books on psychology before he turned out to be one of the most developed people in America. Feed your passion. Initially you may not have anything to show for it but don't stop. People may think you are crazy but don't give up. You are awakening great changes in you. Feed till your mind starts to moult, feed till your character starts to evolve. There is something in you that you are calling out. You are beckoning on transformation and conjuring metamorphosis.

METAMORPHOSIS

For a caterpillar to reach its destiny, it must undergo a process called metamorphosis when its old body undergoes remarkable transformation. A caterpillar then moves to another stage of life called the pupa also known as chrysalis; this is when a caterpillar is enclosed inside a cocoon sack. Nobody on the outside knows what goes on inside the cocoon yet inside there the tissues, limbs and organs of a caterpillar undergo remarkable changes.

You need a metamorphosis. It may be a mental metamorphosis where you moult off old habits, ideologies, and idiosyncrasies, and philosophies. It may be a spiritual metamorphosis where you moult off your old spiritual nature or physical metamorphoses where you burn some fats, shed some weights and lose some pounds to stay healthy and fit.

Old clothes don't fit again because you have outgrown them so are old ideologies, philosophies and relationship that are outdated. Metamorphosis is when you upgrade yourself mentally, physically and spiritually, as well as stay updated with trends that enhance your effectiveness.

Metamorphosis is when you cut off from what and who distracts you, and focus on developing yourself. It is a place of personal retreat. It is a place where you disengage from unproductive activities; pay the price in unseen quiet places. It is a place of solitude, reflection, rejuvenation and revelation. Metamorphosis is when you unlearn, learn and relearn. It is when you plan and re-plan your life. Adjust your focus and re-strategize your system. Edit your old private principles and philosophies that are no longer effective.

There are people who think they have seen the best of you and nothing more to expect from you. Tell them, "Stay tuned. You've not seen anything yet." The best chapter of your life is not written yet. And the best gift you should give yourself is to keep developing till your sack cracks. And when your sacks, definitely you will know.

EMERGENCE

Your sack has cracked! I can hear it as I am writing this paragraph. It is time to come out of your cocoon. Your potential and destiny can't stay hidden forever. The world is waiting to see you. The stages are set. The cameras are fixed. The curtain is drawn. The lights are on. Climb the stage. Like a butterfly you are wearing the right costume. The audience wants to be thrilled by your emergence. Fans are waiting to chant your name. Artists are waiting to capture and paint your beauty. Rise, reach for your niche.

You are no longer a caterpillar or a worm; you are now an awe inspiring butterfly - Beautiful and adorable; magnificent and colourful. Who will not admire you? They will look in admiration as you fly around and dazzle their eyes in the television. They will be spell bond at the sound of your voice. Those that once detested you will admire you. Those that insulted you will marvel at your result. You may not be a high flyer as eagle but you are a beauty to this wonderful world, don't ever forget that.

When you emerge from the cocoon, there is something special about you that you must notice which was not there before: Wings - Your ability to fly. It is our ability to move from where you are to where you want to be. At this moment, people begin to notice you. You no longer wiggle through life in obscurity, but your life as a celebrity begins. People now know about you. They ask for your services. They buy your products. They come for your show or host you in their show. Companies want to sign you up in an endorsement. At this time, old things are passed away all things are becoming new. So it is your time to fly. Are you ready to fly?

CHAPTER 4.

FLY

Have you ever thought about flying? I mean have you ever thought about reaching a great height in life? Have you ever imagined yourself in a high place in life? If Yes, then your time has come.

Those inclinations, imaginations and thoughts are clear signs that you are destined to fly. The sky is calling. Greatness is calling. So get ready to fly. There is an instinct in you that is calling you to embrace your destiny despite how you doubt yourself.

Flightless birds like penguin and ostrich don't have the instinct to fly. No matter what the eagle says to convince them to fly they can't. No amount of motivational message can make them to fly because it is not their destiny. The destiny of penguin is in the sea, she prefers staying in her island with family and friends, then go for fishing every now and then. She is a great swimmer who can swim very fast in the water by flapping her wing like fin.

At the other end is an ostrich with his long legs. It is one of the fastest birds on ground; he enjoys staying in dry grounds. Eagle cannot compete with it in a race on plain lands neither can eagle challenge a penguin to a swimming competition. They are their best in their different niches. There's no competition in destiny as they say, so don't compare yourself with anyone. Ostriches and Penguins don't want to be famous or be celebrities. They don't care about the glamour of excellence. That's who they are and it doesn't make them failures in anyway.

I remember having a chit-chat with one of my classmate in my university days. We were sharing our long time goals. While I was telling him about how I want to have international influence and I was shocked when he said that none of that moves him. He said he doesn't want to be famous or great. He said if he would be doing a nice paying job, with a good family then everything would be okay for him. I was surprised that such an intelligent guy would say that, I didn't get it then until recently that I begin to realize that some people are not destined to fly, they like being grounded and maintain a low profile. It doesn't make them a failure; it is their destiny to live a quiet life in a quiet way.

Your niche is to soar the air and none can compete with you in what you are called to do in life. Don't try to compete with someone with a different destiny and be compared to any of them. Stop trying to convince your friends to join your course they may be of a different destiny. And no matter how you try to convince them to fly, achieve some certain things and reach some certain heights they will never see the need to because they are not destined to fly.

Like the song by R. Kelly above- Do you believe you can fly? Do you believe that you can act a movie, compete in a world sports competition, design a great master piece or edifice, invent something never seen before, entertain a huge audience, lead an organization successfully, paint mind blowing pictures, sing bestselling songs, write an award winning books? Do you think it every night and day? Why not spread your wings, add actions to your passions and fly away?

Flying is expressing yourself, your gifts and your talents to the amazement or benefit of onlookers. That's something in you that you need to express excellently and positively.

THE THREE AIRWAYS

The first airway is the called the Direct Airline. It is the airway of the eagle that grew up in her mother eagle's nest. She learns to fly under the tutorship of her eagle mother. When it is time to leave the nest and fly, the mother eagle makes the nest uncomfortable for her to stay. She removes the grass layer in the nest that brings about comfort and leave the uncomfortable layer that is full of thorns, thistles and pricking twigs that would make the nest an uncomfortable place for the eaglet to stay.

If life is very comfortable for you, you may not fly. If you are a pampered princess who basks under the sweet smelling incense of easiness, you may not fly. If you get what you want whenever you want it, you may not see the need to go out there to hunt. And you may not consider flying because you see food to eat, clothes to wear and a place to sleep. You will prefer to sit on your soft sofa surfing your phone. But when life becomes uncomfortable, it pushes you to fly. Adverse situations can push you out of your comfort zone towards the place you are destined to be. So watch out, when people who used to invite you starts to fight you; when the one who hatched you starts to hurt you; when the ones you stick around with starts to pick on you; when people who used to hear you out starts to tear you apart; when a friend starts to become a fiend and love becomes hate. Don't take it personal. It's a way life is pushing you out of the nest to nature. It is a signal that you should move from where you are to where you should be. You may keep resisting it until life pushes you off the edge then you will have no option than to fly.

When you graduate from being an eaglet to become a flyable young eagle, parent eagle will teach you to fly by picking you out of the nest, carry you up to the sky and drop you to apply the lessons they have been teaching you since the day you were born. Trust me, mentors know when best to release you to start your own. When they know the time is right, they release you to start your own life, business, career, ministry. At this stage, they are pushing you to your independence, they don't want to assist you as they used to, they don't want to come to your aid always as when you had no wings. They just drop you from off the sky and let you figure it out on how to fly on your own.

You may think they are being mean but they are not. They are showing you tough love. They believe in you. They know you can fly. They know you are now matured enough to handle the affairs of life, the challenges of success, and discover your own style of flying. All you need to do is to believe in yourself.

Initially you will struggle to maintain balance, you will struggle to maintain focus, struggle to have a flow, struggle to find your own rhythm and style. You fly from one branch to another then perch to rest and strategize. Give it time, you will figure it out. Tell yourself, 'I'll get it with time.' They will not watch you fall to your destruction; they will catch you before you crash and repeat the exercise till you get it.

The second airway is an Indirect Airline; it is the airway of the eagle that grew up among chickens. It didn't know exactly what it was until the day a father eagle appeared on the sky. The chickens ran for their safety but not the young eaglet this time. It found connection in the cry of the parent eagle. The more the father eagle called out the more it felt stirred on the inside.

It discovered that it looked more like the creature up in the sky and sounded more like it than the chickens it grew up with. The bill was big, yellow and curved. The craws were long and sharp alike. The feathers were huge and wide. It thought within itself, "If that creature up there could do it, so should I." It spread its wings and throws itself into the air. The more it flapped its wings the more it saw itself rising high and so it soared into a higher life. The chicken siblings, turkey friends and other related birds were looking up in amazement. They began to say to each other, "You see that guy up there? I know him very well, he used to be my friend."

Another said: "We grew up together."

"Yea, he was my brother from a different mother." Another interrupted.

The debate doesn't matter again. The eaglet escaped the life he didn't belong to.

It's time for you to escape a life you don't belong to. As much as you try to blend in, as much as you try to get them to like you and fit in with them, you will always feel lost. Something inside of you will keep telling you, you don't belong with them. You notice you stand outstanding each time you are standing with them. When you dress like them, you appear distinct, even people tell you that you are different. When people tell you that you are different, take it as a compliment not the reason to wallow in self-pity. Don't let the approval of others become more important that your own self approval. Have the courage to accept who you are despising what others say or think about you.

You live with them but you don't know why you always feel that you will leave them one day to a better place. Then a day comes, that you come across a book that communicates to you, a preacher that sounds like he saw you in your secret closet, a teacher that connects to your style of learning, a song that brings out your wonderful voice, an artist or actor you want to be like, an athlete who is the best version of your immature self, the man or woman whose name stirs you up, an organization or profession where you feel at home, then everything starts to make sense and the answer to the questions you have been asking for years becomes clear.

It is your time and your moment. Take it! Don't you

procrastinate your destiny this time and don't accuse yourself with excuses. Don't listen to chickens, you have scratched the ground enough with them. You have gossiped and squawked loud enough with them. Stop trying to convince them to fly; they won't. Stop trying to get them to join you they don't have the same destiny with you. Stop trying to make them see the visions you saw; their vision is very shallow. They may not support your career or business ideas. Don't be angry with them, they are not seeing what you saw. It's time for you to spread your wings, flap them and throw yourself into the air.

I know you didn't have a mentor earlier on in life who gave you the right foundations. You didn't have a sponsor who would have provided you with needful resources. You didn't have a parent eagle around to teach you the ways of a high flyer yet you have the potentials. Keep watching, listening and modeling your role models, one day you will play your role well and become like them. You can be like that man you listen to. You can be like that woman you always watch on the television. You can be like the celebrity you read about and follow on the social media. If they could do it, so can you. The ability is in you just respond to it. Observing them can inspire what lies in you because greatness inspires greatness. Excellence inspires excellence. Effective leadership inspires more effective leadership. Model bigger eagles. Don't worry about people who mock you that you can never get it right like them. Soon they will watch you rise and soar.

The third airway is called the Awkward Airline; it is the airline of a caterpillar who became a butterfly. After the sack cracked, the butterfly emerged from the cocoon with folded soft wings She was not born with wings but along the line by training she develops some wings, very beautiful wings and she must fly with them. She has to wait for like four hours to pump blood into the wings in order to get them working and flapping. After the wings have received enough blood, the butterfly would start flapping her wings till she starts flying. It takes up to four hours for the butterfly to master flying.

You have acquired a skill but your skill is soft and folded like the wings of a butterfly that newly emerged from chrysalis. You need to pump energy and time to your skills. Tell yourself that you can. Continue telling yourself that you can till your entire system is supercharged and energized to perform. Affirm positively always by doing that you pump energy to your gifts and talents. Invest in whatever you are good at. Invest your energy, money and time. If you fold your abilities, you hold back your destiny. Spread out your wings, flap them, flap them again and again till you are air bound.

Don't expect to get it figured out at once because you have no one to put you through it, you have no role model to emulate. Don't expect to fly one hour in a stretch. Start with 15 minutes' flight, then 30 minutes' flight, 45 minutes' flight then make it 1 hour and more. Don't be too hard on yourself. Give yourself the time to learn and grow. You will get better with time.

You are no longer crawling or wiggling again. Fly even if it means flying in a hazy zig-zag way. Your journey may not be in a straight line. It may be like electrocardiogram wave, up and down, irregular. You may rise today and fall tomorrow. You may get it today and mess it up tomorrow. Be consistent and persistent. If you fall, make sure you rise again. Pick yourself up from the dust when you fall, clean yourself and throw yourself back into the air. Keep trying until you pick and reach the peak.

It takes butterfly 4 hours to master flying. It takes we humans 10,000 hours to master our flying in any field we choose. Just listen to the conclusion of neurologist Daniel Levitin made: "*After numerous studies we come to see the following rule: whatever field one chooses to achieve, the level of skill commensurate with the status of a world-class expert, it requires 10,000 hours of practice. No matter whom you take – composers, basketball players, writers, skaters, pianists, chess players and inveterate criminals and soon – we meet this figure with asurprising regularity. Ten thousand hours means approximately three hours of practice per day, or twenty hours per week for the past ten years. Yet there is not a single case of a person who achieved the highest level of skill in a less period of time."*

YOU AGAINST THE WORLD

If you crawl like a green snake in green grasses, all eyes may not see you but if you fly like an eagle under a bright blue sky or like a beautiful butterfly on a garden of colourful flowers, believe me attentions will be on you. Anything that flies attracts attention and expectations. If you are destined to fly all eyes will be on you yet you are not Tupac Shakur. People will watch every step you take; each post you make on social media. They will analyze and criticize every move you make. They may want to take your privacy away from you by implying into some sensitive areas of your life. Are you ready to handle such level of attention?

Some good ones will look up to you and their expectations of you will be high always. The pressure to live up to their expectations can be too much that at a certain point you become conscious of pleasing them than living the life you are created to live, because you know that if you slip in anyway criticisms will come. And I know how much you hate criticism and how much you hate disappointing anyone. Are you ready to live up to people's expectations?

Some people may not be comfortable with you being yourself. They don't want to see you fly over their heads, they prefer to shoot you out of the sky and have you caged somewhere. Don't allow anyone's opinion of you stop you from being yourself. As a social butterfly you are destined to be an epitome of social beauty and elegance. As an eagle you are destined to be a symbol of excellence, leadership, freedom and power. You owe no one an explanation of who you are. Feel free to be yourself.

If you think you can't handle attention and expectations of people, it is because you are afraid of their abuses, blackmails, criticisms, disses, hate and gossip. Be ready, people will cast their harsh stones of criticism, their arrows of gossips, and bullets of blackmail at you. They will hurl their catapult of rejection and canons of court cases at you. Get ready, blogs, fake friends, magazines, newspapers and tabloids will come at you but don't let anyone or anything shoot you off the sky. Dodge their arrows and bullets. Wear the protective vest of 'I don't give a damn' to survive what they do and say. Even if they say you are not bright and colourful enough, not educated enough, not good enough, not pretty enough, not smart enough, not talented enough. If you allow it hit you hard, recovering from it won't be easy.

As an eagle people who fly with you can fight you as well. They can attack you from your back as crows do attack eagles. Crow is one bird that dares to peck at an eagle. He flies up to an eagle sits on his back and bites his neck. You will expect the eagle to fight back because it is bigger but it does something interesting, it chooses not to waste its time or energy on the crow. It chooses to rise higher into the heavens, the higher the flight the harder it is for the crow to follow him because the crow cannot breathe well very at certain altitude due to lack of oxygen.

Choose not to fight with crows. Don't fight anyone who has nothing to lose, no glory to protect, no legacy to preserve and no reputation to uphold. They will come from behind and bite your neck, ignore and pull away from them. Reply insults with results. Reply enemies with more success. Rise to a level where they can't access you. In Nicky Minaj song FLY I like the lines that goes like this:

"Me, me, me, against them

Me against enemies, me against friends

Somehow they both seem to become one

A sea full of sharks and they all smell blood

They start coming and I start rising

Must be surprising, I'm just surmising

I win, thrive, soar, higher, higher, higher

More fire."

When you fly, some people will complain you are an attention seeker who likes showing off, they will accuse you of having excessive cravings for accolade. As a social butterfly, updating your social media status with beauties and witty quotes, some people will find it uncomfortable. Some will despise you because you don't perch on a little branch by the window of people's life and chirp gossips with them as little morning birds. Some people will feel irritated for the fact that they can't have hundred percent hold on you because you float like a butterfly and sting like a bee. They will resent you because you don't show up all the time and you're very picky with where you go and people you are seen with just like eagles do. Isn't that crazy?

Don't worry about people who are allergic to you, you don't belong with them, focus on people who need and value your honey. Take your graceful presence to where you are celebrated not where you are tolerated. Focus on perching on sweet smelling flowers not on foul stinking weeds. Remember, it's not every colourful sweet smelling places and persons you should be with because some attract you to trap you like carnivorous flowers. So don't be trapped by anybody's affection.

DON'T BE AFRAID TO FLY

When we were little boys, growing up in a village with a beautiful natural setting, we used to catch young hatchlings under a tree. Some of those little birds were birds who fell off the sky while trying to fly and got wounded in the process. While holding them in our tiny hands we could see the fear in their eyes. Sometimes it could be a fear to try another flight. Some of us loved to keep those little chicks and feed them but I was among those who had the opinion of sending them back to the air because we've had bad experiences of watching those little beautiful creatures die in our cage because we didn't have the quality of a mother bird to give them what they wanted when they wanted them.

It was always fun trying to help them fly again by throwing them up into the air. If you tried something and failed, you may have the fear of not trying another time. Sustaining emotional wounds from your first attempts can crush your zeal to continue. You are convinced that you can fly but you are afraid of sustaining more hurts by trying harder. For example, you launched a program and it clashed, you acted or shot a movie and the rating was poor, you wrote a book, released a music album, started a business that failed before your face, you staged a show and the attendance turnover was too poor. It has a way of demoralizing you because you know the energy you used to try to fly in the first place. But don't give up.

I understand the acrophobia and aerophobia. When you see a plane crash you may develop the fear of flight. If you see life from the eyes of famous people who have fallen from grace you may not want to be famous again. If you overlook the glamour of the things they enjoy and take an objective look at the horror of things they pass through to stay afloat, you may be scared to your bone. When you begin to see what it takes to sustain success and pressures that follows maintaining someone's fame. You may get discouraged.

It doesn't matter who you were yesterday, they want to know who you are today. They no longer care about what you did yesterday they are after what you can deliver today. They don't want to hear that you lack inspiration, that you had a mental block. Every week they will stay tuned to hear you say something or watch you perform because they feed on your creativity. Even after the curtains close the show goes on for you, because life at the back stage can be exhausting. You are under constant pressure to perform and deliver. They always want to see you in form. They won't tolerate bad form. If you sustain an injury, treat it and recover with the speed of light. If you don't they will send you to oblivion. You must crop out your failures and flaws and project perfections. They don't mind if you wear a perfect mask, just come out perfect because that's what they want to see. They lift you to a slippery pedestal that if you are not careful, you fall to your destruction. And the higher you go the more unforgiving they are if you trip. They idolize you so why won't you be perfect. If you slip, then you face the rhythm of scandal and court cases. Phew! Nobody wants to fly just to fall off the sky of fame.

This is a world where if your face appears in the newspaper or magazine, it will automatically take you to the lime light and give you huge followership. Then if your face appears again with the wrong caption, you feel like one shot out of the sky. It will come like a dark storm that destroys what you spent years to build. One mistake from you can make them fire you out of your flying position. One careless move can be used to knock you off the stage of fame and fortune. It takes discipline to remain successful. And I know you can remember famous people you used to admire and idolize who were shot off the sky. Sometimes it scares you that you don't want to end up like them.

I once had a fear like that when I lost my most powerful eagle mother, she was knocked out of the sky and she never recovered. I was scared to my bone. She was someone who used to come to my rescue whenever I had a spiritual storm to face. I told myself, "If she could be knocked out with all her power and experience, who am I to try and fly?" For some time in my life, I gave up on destiny and my visions. Until I later rediscovered and reinvented myself again, picked myself up, dust off the depressions and frustrations, exorcised my acrophobia and aerophobia demons, spread my wings for another flight.

I know you must have asked yourself – What if I fall? You tell yourself, 'I don't want to end up as so and so.'

The best thing to do is to learn from the mistakes of those people so that you will not repeat them. Most times great people fall by their own sword and carelessness.

There is a story of an eagle that was shot while flying its way to destiny. The arrow hit it so hard that it couldn't maintain its flight despite how it tried to recover. it fell off the sky and landed on a dusty plain. While it was writhing in pain, it gazed down on the arrow that hit it. it was shocked to notice that its own feather was used in making the shaft of the arrow. That's when it understood that it gave its enemies the means for its own downfall.

Minimize your weaknesses and maximize your strength. Nobody is perfect but try as much as possible not to highlight your imperfections. Protect your blind spot and guard your Achilles heels, if you can't eradicate them entirely. And don't complicate your life with relationships that will implicate your destiny. Fight to survive, but don't pick up the wrong fight that can kill you. Everything and everyone no longer require your attention. Don't focus on what doesn't feed your destiny. Focus on what sustains you. Priorities is not selfishness it is smartness. Pain is acceptable only if it brings you gain.

Excellence is your destiny so take your eyes off mediocrity. Focus on high flyers who refused to be shot out of the sky despite the accusations and criticisms the world throw at them. They keep soaring despite the storm of bankruptcy, court cases and guiltless scandals. They have developed strong hides and tough skins over time. You need to be strong and tough too. Don't let anything they shoot at you hit you. Even if it hits you by mistake, don't let it penetrate and have a hold on you. If you are hurting in anyway try as much as possible to heal fast, recover and bounce back.

Have you ever seen a chicken trying to fly over a high fence? It is always amusing and seriously ridiculous to watch. The chicken will pace to and fro, sit, squat and stand uncountable times. You can see aerophobia written over her chicken face. But eagles have no such phobias. It is its destiny and it has the abilities. If you developed any aerophobia or acrophobia from your chicken friends or siblings. Knock it off.

You are destined to fly stop being afraid of great heights and its pressure. Deal with your fear so that it won't become your greatest enemy. Don't let the fear of the storm stop you. Eagles are best in handling the storm because the eagle sets his wing in such a way that the wind will pick him and lift him above the storm. In most cases eagles fly above the storm, so instead of escaping the storm they use the storm to rise higher. The storm can come and I believe you can handle it because what doesn't kill you makes you stronger.

In life, you have a far distance to cover and you must know when and where to spend your energy in this journey. When eagles are flying far distance they know how to conserve their energy by following the thermal current of warm air to soar. They position themselves high in a thermal current and glide downwards or upward to catch the next current.

Learn how to follow the warm currents of muse and powerful inspirations to maintain your flow. Musicians know that the warm current of muse can come while you are in the bathroom or in the middle of the night. Writers know the current can come while sitting in a serene environment, travelling or yachting. Artists can pick it while sitting down by a river side admiring the beauties of nature. Actors can get inspired by interpreting little things transpiring around them. The warm current doesn't come every day or hour. The scenes you see around you can create a great story for you. The surrounding sounds in your streets made by inanimate objects can whisper sweet songs in your eyes. Creativity is like a warm wave, set your creative antenna to pick the thermal currents of muse when they come, follow the current each time you sense it, it will help you to flow better than always struggling to fly with hazy ideas.

What I am trying to say is this: if you have the grace to do or achieve something at a certain time in your life, utilize and maximize it, don't let it pass you by. The unction to function doesn't come all the time.

BIRDS OF A FEATHER

Finally, I advise you, don't be a lone ranger. Join a team of high flyers. Eagles don't always fly alone they know how to link up with themselves especially during winter seasons. They fly in the company of each other. Join a team that will support you and help you overcome the fear of doing it alone. A team of two to three eagles help a lot. Where two or three eagles gather in the name of creativity, greatness is always in their midst. Form an aerie and build your own eyrie.

A team of Plantation Boys brought out an eagle like Innocent 'Tu-Baba' Idibia, one of the most successful Nigerian singers. In the same way, a team of Destiny Child brought out Beyoncé Knowles.

The team of Barcelona Football club brought the great Lionel Messi who emerged from the nest of La Masia football academy. The Chicago Bulls basketball team brought out the great Michael Jordan who is a basketball icon and by acclamation the greatest basketball player of all time.

As you are a singer, if you can't start singing alone, start with a musical band. If you can't write a book on your own you can co-author with another wonderful writer. As a painter, when you paint you need the eyes of another artist to make it balance. As an athlete parring with another athlete sharpens you like an iron. If you are a scientist, you can join a club of smart scientist to stay updated. Nerds move with nerds. Artists move with artists. Entertainers are always seen in the company of one of another. Locate your kind and join feathers with them.

CHAPTER 5.

ON TOP OF THE WORLD

One day, your life will be like a fairytale with a happy ending. Can I get a smile from you? When life has given you everything you have ever dreamed and imagined you will be glad that you pecked your way out of the restricting shell to unstuck yourself. You will be happy that you waited patiently in the nest to grow and develop without rushing things. You will be thankful to those who gave you warmth, covered you from cold, rain and heat with their affection while you were still helpless in the nest. You will also be thankful to those who made the nest uncomfortable for you and pushed you out to your own destiny. You will be proud that you parted ways with your flightless chicken friends and peer groups.

One day you will be grateful that you endured and survived the frustrating life of a worm. You didn't allow haters and mockers to crush you but persisted and fed on what made you grow till you metamorphosed. You will look back at all the challenges, failures, disappointments, rejections, broken hearts, rise and fall in your journey so far, you will reflect on how far you have come then you will be grateful to God your maker.

One day you will be on top of the world where money will no longer be your problem because you can afford whatever you want to have, buy anything that interests you, sponsor yourself on a vacation to anywhere on earth that you desire to go because you have the freedom. One day you will sit back and enjoy the reward of success and still run your business from anyway in the world because location and its allocations will no longer be problem. You will lodge in any hotel suite of your choice with an ocean view. You will relax in a Caribbean beach and surf in the waves. You will sleep and wake up whenever you want because you are your own boss.

When you enter the street you will nod in fulfilment as you hear people playing your music in their radio, stereo and MP3. You will smile at the giant picture of you on a huge bill board. When you turn on the television you will be watching yourself or watch people talking about you. You will get emails of appreciations and questions from people around the world who read your books and they are positively imparted by them. And when you grace the stage to perform, thousands and millions will be screaming your name they will welcome you with rounds of applause, standing ovations and unending flashes of camera lights as you walk the red carpet. You will be inducted in the Hall of Fame of stars. You will have huge fan base in social media platforms.

Being an epitome of social beauty, companies will like you to be their brand ambassador, make you the face of their reputable firm. And being a symbol of leadership, organizations and institutions will clamour to have you lead and represent them.

One day you will look at your success, reflect back on your journey as a high flyer and say, "So I'm finally here. I can't believe I made it and achieved this."

Let your heart be full of gratitude because it is only the attitude of gratitude that can sustain you in a high altitude of life.

When you come to that stage of your life when you feel you

are on top of the world. There are two mistakes you should be careful not to make.

<u>When You Become Great, Don't Neglect Your Family And Friends:</u> I believe family and friends are those you choose to take as family and friends because some people don't worth it. Someone is not your family because your grandfather's blood that runs in your vein runs in his as well. They are your family because you share common love, faith and destiny with them. So be wise with who you accept as family. When you succeed share your success with your family and friends. When you fly, lift them to fly with you unless they don't want to fly alongside you. You can't force anyone to fly with you. There's more security in flying with them than flying alone because you need someone to watch your back unless they are out to antagonize you and bring about your downfall. If you can, meet their needs. Reward those who helped and supported you on your way up. You can't rise and despise them. A true eagle shares the meat he got from hunting with his family and friends. If they don't have a resting nest, help them build one. In fact, family are the reason why you succeeded in the first place because you may be the only one destined to be the eagle of your family who will lift them out of their poor predicament. Don't forget that. Fame is fickle and the day it fizzles away, where will you go back to?

<u>Don't Let Your Passion Become Pride Rather Turn It To Compassion:</u> When you find yourself flying high in life, don't let it get into your head. The fact that people allow you fly over their head should not make you to perch on their head nor does it license you to shit on their head and make your nest on them. They will never allow you to do that. Rather perch on their shoulder and give them glory. Everyone wants an eagle on their shoulder because of the honour it brings, give them that honour and power to have you in their life. If they stretch forth their hand to you, perch on them. There's a lot you will help them do and achieve. If they ask you for your feather, give the ones that deserve it to put it on their cap. Give no place to pride because pride is a cancer that eats up high flyers. Passion will get you to wherever you want to be but compassion will sustain you there. Whenever you look down from the pinnacle of your success, don't always see a prey to catch, see a baby eagle stuck with chickens that you should help. Remember where you came from, the shell where you were once stuck, someone is stuck in a similar shell too, and it is also your destiny to help them peck their way out. Remember your life with chickens in the neighbourhood, some eaglets are lost to their destiny, call out to them and help them realize who they are just like you did. Help them break of the cage holding them.

CAGED BIRD

One day, during a break time from work, I and my friend drove down to a Polo park. While my friend was busy with an official call over the phone. I was busy sight-seeing, enjoying the scene until my eyes saw an error under the sun.

I saw a very big bird in a cage and beside the cage is a chicken scratching the ground to the annoyance of the big bird. I went closer and I couldn't believe my eyes. It was an eagle in that cage. Actually it was my first time to see an eagle in real life. The vendor told me the eagle was for sale just like every other animal there – monkeys, parrots, peacock, different kinds of bird, dogs and turtles. It shocked me to see an eagle stuck in a cage but a chicken was free bragging around the cage. It makes me to wonder how many eagles are caged in life. So many great destinies are caged. While those who have lesser worth are busy enjoying what high flyers should be enjoying.

Have you seen someone who has so much money but doesn't know exactly what to do with the money so they waste them, but you know what you can do with such amount of money they squander around. You know where to invest such money if you can lay your hands on them. Sometimes life is not fair that some people squander the opportunities and privileges others pray for. I remember the poem of Maya Angelou - Caged Bird:

'But a caged bird stands on the grave of dreams

In shadow shouts of a nightmare scream

His wings are clipped and his feet are tied

So he opens his throat to sing.'

Isn't it ironic that some birds have aspirations and visions but can't actualize it because they are stuck behind golden or silver bars? They know what to do and where to go but they can't because they are caged, their wings are clipped and their feet tied. They are so confined that they can't express their potentials. They are locked away from the right connections they need to rise behind rusted bars of lack and inexposure. Just as Poetess Maya said in her poem, 'A caged bird stands on the grave of dreams.' Many great eagles are caged behind emotional, financial, social and spiritual bars, and if freedom fails to come, they will die with their dreams.

Some of those eagles didn't start off in the cage, they made a decision and got trapped. Some were seduced into a cage. Some fell in love and found themselves trapped in a romantic cage. They ignorantly gave up their freedom. Some were under pressure to perform in high state that they got trapped in cage of drug addiction and alcoholism. Some were pursued into a cage, while they are running away from bankruptcy and tragic experiences and they were offered a way out which turned out to be a cage.

Be careful when you need what you think you can't handle because hunters will come and make huge offers that you will find it hard to reject. They will offer you a huge price to buy your growing company or franchise that took you years of hard and smart work to build. They will want you to sell your right to a particular product or brand that you cherish so much. They see the future more than you see it because of your level in life. They can offer anything to buy your future and because of your immediate need, but don't sell the future to sustain the present.

Before you realize it you are stuck in a golden cage where you smell golden bars but losses your freedom of creativity and expression. They decide the kind of life you should live and make decisions for you in the name of being your manager.

However, when you are on top of the world don't forget those caged birds who don't enjoy the freedom and excellence that you do. It's your purpose to help them and free them like Nelson Mandela. It is your purpose to reach out to them and give them hope that adverse situations of life have denied them. Life is more than making a living, you need to make a giving and make a difference. Don't forget your kind. You succeed to help your kind succeed not to abandon them. As for your kind, don't just help them, reproduce them.

WHY EAGLES DATE AND MATE

You can give to the world in different ways but the best way is to reproduce yourself. It takes an eagle to birth an eagle. Someone birthed you, it's time for you to birth another after your kind. It doesn't take one to reproduce. It takes two to reproduce.

An eagle dates and mates with a fellow eagle. An eagle doesn't date and mate with fishes no matter how beautiful the fish is because there's no common ground for them to live. I explained this in two of my poems titled 'Eagles Don't Sing' and 'Fatal Love'. The 'Fatal Love' goes as this:

'I was an eagle

In love with a golden fish

Wishing I could swim or wriggle

But was attracted to snares that pish.'

You can't leave the sky and start living in cages and caves because you are in love with someone who is not your kind. Someone can be good to you but not good for you, you must know the difference. Not everyone deserves you, it is not pride to think like that, it is your nature. There's some people you can't just be with; they are nice people but not the right people for your destiny. Let them admire you from afar, crush on you from afar, love you from afar and praise you from afar but don't let them get too close.

They may be your biggest fan, they follow you in all your social media platforms, they comment on your post, they like all your tweets, your pictures are hanging in their room, they have different autographs from you, your name is attached in their works and you are their biggest role model or idol, don't let it move you. Give them the gratitude and respect they deserve but don't descend too low to their level to date and mate with them, it can be a trap and they can be a fatal bait. Stop feeling guilty about who loves you that you fail to love back as long as they are not the right person for you. Some come to use you to rise and shine so it is always hard to see who to trust. If you don't want to ruin your destiny be very picky and selective, that's why you are an eagle.

Female eagle faces many suitors but she is very selective in choosing her mate. She has self-control, so she doesn't rush into any relationship. She takes her time and evaluate them over a period of time, by instinct she chooses the male eagle she will date (fly with for a while).

As they fly around she watches to know if she likes the way he flies. If she likes his ways then she would move to the next level of testing him. She tests him by putting him through series and stages of tests by picking up a stick or twig then flies high with it and drops it, she then watches her male suitor to know if he can catch it and bring it back to her. Then she repeats the same exercise by carrying a bigger stick and flies to a higher altitude. The male eagle must prove himself to her over and over again that he is a worthy mate.

As an eagle you need a worthy mate because your destiny is far and high and you need someone who will be with you to that distance and height. It is one's destiny to be an eagle, it's another's destiny to be the eagle's mate. Find your mate, your destiny depends on it. You test him or her before you trust them with your destiny. You need to know if they catch you when you fall, will they give you their wings when you lose yours. If they fail the test, they don't deserve you and don't be sentimental about it. Move on and don't look back. The right one awaits you somewhere.

Relationship has a way of giving and supporting you. Self-love is good but someone's love can do a lot for you as well. They will help you scratch under the feathers. They will help scratch where you may not reach to scratch yourself. Relationship helps refuel you. Love and be loved. Give love and allow yourself to receive love. The love of your fans and followers are far away love, you need someone you love and trust close to your heart.

When you find the right one, start a family, a relationship or a team that will reproduce more high flyers into this wonderful world. You must continue the circle so that the lineage of high flyers won't go extinct. Reproduce more successful people under you. Reproduce people with great gifts and talents under you. Success is not complete without a successor.

Build your nest where eaglets will hatch out, it may be a club, a foundation, a ministry, an outreach, a non-governmental organization (NGO), a rehabilitation center, a school; let it be a nursery through which excellence and greatness is hatched into this world.

Just as a butterfly brings balance to nature, you must do more than sucking sweet nectars of fame and making the world a colourful place by beautifying the eyes of people that watch you in the television or cinema screams. It is not enough to dazzle the fantasy of millions on the stages of entertainment as a beauty queen, you pollinate the society with love, peace and unity. You must be an agent of happiness.

RETIRE OR RE-FIRE

As a high flyer you will come to a point in your life when you think you have seen it all and you have given your best. At that moment after you have seen the world and tasted the rewards of fame and success. You have the option to retire or rest and re-fire later.

Many chooses to retire and spend the rest of their life playing golf and yachting the seas. While some chooses to remove themselves from public eyes, retire to oblivion in an Island to spend more time with their family. But there are people who out of passion wants to continue giving back to the world because they want to stay relevant till death. If you belong to the later you can learn from this story of an eagle that has a rebirth. The story is fiction without any scientific backings but I believe you can learn wonderful lessons from it.

The eagle has the longest life-span among birds. It can live up to 70 years. but to reach this age, the eagle must make a hard decision. In its 40's its long and flexible talons can no longer grab prey which serves as food. Its long and sharp beak becomes bent. Its old-aged and heavy wings, due to their thick feathers, become stuck to its' chest and make it difficult to fly. Then the eagle is left with only two options: DIE or go through a painful process of change which lasts 150 days. The process requires that the eagle fly to a mountain top and sit on its nest. There the eagle knocks its beak against a rock until it plucks it out. When its new talons grow back, the eagle starts plucking its old-aged feathers. And after five months, the eagle takes its famous flight of rebirth and lives for 30 more years. – **Anonymous.**

Now let's focus on the moral lesson of the story above. When you reach that point in your life when you think you are old, tired and weak, you can choose to be reborn. You have to let go of your glory days and focus on a new glory you want to create.

When you think you have seen it all, you have achieved it all, no more places to go, no more distances to cover or far heights to reach, you are limiting yourself because there are so much more to do.

There is more beyond your present level or position in life.

There is more beyond your present state of health, more beyond your present financial income or net worth. There is more beyond being famous and winning awards. So don't say 'This is it' until destiny is totally actualized and fulfilled. The chapters of your live is not complete until there are no more pages to write.

History recorded that Alexander the Great was angry when they told him there were no more world to conquer, but his advisors lied to him. There is more world to conquer, more mountains to climb, more rivers to cross. So rest and re-fire one more time.

At this stage, old way of doing things may not work again. Old methods and strategies may be outdated so you need to knock them off, update and upgrade yourself. Old tactic may get blunt and you need a new one. Your need a reborn, you need to stage your come back and take the world one more time till you have given your all.

Remember you are a high flyer. Live as one. See you at the top. As a high flyer I want you play or sing this song every morning, it will serve as your morning wake up coffee to get you ready for the day. It is Nicky Minaj song 'Fly':

I came to win, to fight, to conquer, to thrive

I came to win, to survive, to prosper, to rise

To fly

To fly

ABOUT THE AUTHOR

Chidi C. Obigod

 Chidi C. ObiGod is a human development and relationship life coach, a motivational speaker, writer and poet. He has written life transforming books like You Can Be What You Want To Be, I Have A Dream, Don't Wash Your Net Yet, Dangerous Damsels, Prince Harming etc.

9 798691 468117